Words of wisdom
Practical Tips on How to be Successful, Happy and Loved

Benjamin Wood

Introduction

Thank you for purchasing this book it is my sincere hope that it will answer all your questions. The most important point of practicing self-ness is that when you are whole and well you are not the only one who reaps the benefits. This holistic way of living your life is beneficial to all within your sphere. It has a healthy domino effect. Like the abundant spread of wildflowers in meadows, the seeds from self-ness will subtly bring their beauty to everyone in your life. Reading nourishes the soul and mind. Begin feeding yourself now; please read on.

Table of Contents

THE PARABLES

1. Mirror-Image: Your Mirror, Your Image

"I turned and saw a lovely woman whose eyes seemed kind. With a shock, I realized I was looking at a reflection in a store window and the woman was me! It was amazing because I never liked looking in mirrors, always finding fault with myself! I always thought other women looked better than I did. By unexpectedly seeing myself for one minute without a critical eye, I saw a whole new me, and I liked what I saw."

~ Kate Winslet, actor

Do you regularly find fault with yourself because you feel you don't "match-up" to other people? When you are always comparing yourself in another person's mirror, negative thoughts begin to take hold. You need to remember that your unique life's journey isn't anybody else's journey, it is solely yours.

The image you see in the mirror every day is you. You can't walk one step without taking "you" with you. Isn't it a good idea to enjoy being with yourself? Be a best friend to yourself. Remember that you care about the person in the mirror and want the best for her.

There is positive criticism, and there is negative criticism. Negative criticism is destructive; it destroys confidence and self-esteem. What you are doing when you allow that critic living inside your mind to be unleashed is as hurtful as the worst type of bullying you can encounter from someone else.

You are bullying yourself by saying that you're not pretty, not smart, not the correct weight, not good enough. If you want to make improvements in your appearance or your life, do so, but do it kindly. Positive criticism is constructive; it builds on the good aspects you already have. All of us have liked the way we look at least sometimes. There is a beauty in all of us that we need to find and cultivate. We are all diverse, and each one of us is unique. Look objectively at yourself and find something in this mirror-image to like. Then look again and find something to love. Let your image reflect a happy well-loved person who knows her self-worth.

Nourishing Thought:
"Look in the mirror... See yourself - Be yourself - Love yourself!" ~ Drew Barrymore, actor Treat you like the precious, unique creation you are. Be your own best friend.

2. Your Happiness, Your Responsibility

"You're responsible for your happiness. Why would you want to give that responsibility to anyone else?"

~ Hilary Rodham Clinton, Secretary of State **No one should have the responsibility** of making and keeping you happy. Depending on others for happiness will be an elusive, fruitless quest. You will be confined to the moods and whims of another, and you will never find happiness living like that.

Explore what does make you happy; what brings a smile to your face. Decide what positive things make you feel good. Bring happiness to yourself by doing what you love. Don't give away your potential for joy by waiting for someone else to "make" you happy. Your life and your happiness are gifts to be cared for and treasured. Why would you throw away these precious gifts?

Who knows you better than you know yourself? No one. Therefore it is irresponsible to expect someone else to "make" you happy. Happiness is not something you can "get," it is there in your inner self just waiting for you to discover and nurture it. Being happy is not a chore, it is a pleasure and your right. Create your happiness and nurture it over the years.

Nourishing Thought:
"No one is in control of your happiness but you; therefore, you have the power to change anything about yourself or your life that you want to change."

~ Barbara de Angelis, motivational speaker Be responsible for creating and finding your joy, and you will be happy

3. The Comfort Zone of Living Well

By living well, you give yourself the advantage of being a healthier person, both emotionally and physically. Individuals who live well not only are happier and able to give to themselves, they are people that others like to be around. They make great friends. When you are contented, it creates a ripple effect in your life and the lives of those close to you. Happiness is contagious.

You deserve to live well and to create a comfort zone of peace for yourself. A small area in your home where you can recharge your energy every day is a necessity. One woman I know has created her comfort zone in the corner of her kitchen. She bought a used desk, puts fresh flowers on it every week, has a small book stand, and sits and reads there each evening for at least twenty minutes. In this zone, she feels cherished and cared-for.

Your comfort zone, wherever you may have it, says that your health and life are held to be precious. You give your spiritual nourishment to grow.
"The beauty of life is living well," means that not only do you make your own life comfortable but that you bring that sense of peace and beauty with you wherever you go. Knowing that you had a sanctuary within where you are comfortable and cared for creates harmony in a chaotic world.

Nourishing Thought:
"The days are the sum of our lives. So live well today for this is what your life story is about." ~ Cale Chew inspirational artist Make living well a priority. Create peace, harmony, and beauty in the world around you.

4. Make Sure You're Okay First

"Attention passengers-In case of emergency, fasten your oxygen mask securely in place over your nose and mouth before assisting others."

Pre-flight safety directions required of all airlines

This is the most sensible statement ever made. How can you take care of anyone else if you're not okay? Being tired, hungry, or overworked helps no one, least of all you. Apply this statement to daily living and see what a difference it makes.

Our society subconsciously dictates that we should take care of everyone else before we even think to take care of ourselves. While helping others is a beautiful and noble endeavor, it should never be done at the expense of your well-being.

Great philanthropists don't stop enjoying their own lives. They live it well. Successful people make taking care of themselves a priority, yet they still perform great charitable acts. By putting themselves first, they are in a position to do much more for others.

Here's a good question to ask when you are running yourself ragged trying to take care of the needs of everyone else:
If you needed help, who would you choose to serve your needs best; the person who is tired, overwhelmed and hadn't taken care of herself or the person who cares for herself, is mentally alert, and in good physical health?
Obviously, you would choose the latter, no question. That person exudes success and confidence in all ways. You would feel safe and confident in your choice because you would know practical, realistic help was available from someone who could provide it well.

Nourishing Thought:
"Remember this: you are your own best friend, so you'd better take care of yourself first." ~ Super Girl Be a lucky person; make you your number one priority.

5. A Closed Door Can Lead to Reinvention

If you constantly look with longing at that which has ended, you will miss seeing the path for fresh and happy experiences. There are many doors in life; why waste time banging on one that is closed to you?

Too many times we cannot "let go" of a situation or relationship. We don't want to believe that a door has been shut in our faces and we bang on that door until our knuckles are bloody. The closed door won't open. We know this, but we still keep beating on it.

Suzanne Farrell was one of the premiere ballerinas of his day. Her body flowed with the music, and her performances were heralded as masterpieces. She had an unusually long performing career for a ballerina. But after 28 years of an occupation which takes a tremendous physical toll on the body she developed arthritis in her right hip and, despite two years of different treatments, she finally put an end to her rigorous schedule of performing. In doing so, she closed the door of her illustrious career.

But even as the one door closed, she found another door opening; the creation of her own dance company. Here she trains new talent and it became a professional goal that she found she loved doing. The excellent addition to this new life is that, because she no longer has the constant physical grind of full-time dancing, she can perform twice a year at select companies where her graceful movements are still a vision of beauty.

Suzanne Farrell was able to accept the closing of one door and dared to see the possibilities of a new door opening for her.
Seek out new paths to travel. Letting go of the old can be a fantastic chance to see your life in a new light and discover new possibilities and choices.

Nourishing Thought:
"There's more to be feared from closed minds than from closed doors. Reinvent yourself."

~ Frank Tyger, columnist You have more than one talent. Open your thoughts and reinvent yourself throughout your entire life.

6. Friendship

"Life without a friend is like a sky without the sun; desolate and cold."~ Anonymous, All creatures on earth, **are sociable**.Even the proverbial lone wolf seeks the companionship of its kind fifty percent of the time.

Loneliness fosters unhappiness. Oh, sure, of course, we do need solitude; being by yourself sometimes is normal and healthy. But it is also a fact that we all need to share our lives with select others. Being alone all the time leads to depression and a feeling of being lost. Those who have jobs that require very little social interaction during the work day, report more job dissatisfaction than workers who socially connect at work.
Statistics have shown that people who socialize live longer and are healthier and happier than those who have no company but their own. Medical doctors have linked loneliness to many health problems and diseases. It is a combination of the mind, body, and spirit all working together that create optimum health. Friendship performs many functions for us. It helps to alleviate sadness, helps us cope with problems, and make us feel not so alone in our world. It is a healing relationship.
A good friend is a gift. Open yourself up to new acquaintances and friendships. Good friends enhance your life. You don't have to be a social butterfly with "fifty BFFs;" one or two good friends are all it takes to feel a part of the human community.

Nourishing Thought:
"A friend is one who walks in when the rest of the world walks out." ~ Walter Winchel, reporter Let sunshine fill your life. Make at least one good friend.

7. Hatred: A Waste of Life

"You lose a lot of time, hating people." ~ Marian Anderson, classical vocalist

How do we feel after an emotional moment? If the emotion is positive, like love and joy, we feel exhilarated and uplifted. But negative emotions, such as hate, can drain our very life-force. Hatred uses a lot of energy and turns the hater into a victim of his or her own emotion. It is a self-defeating action which uses up too much of life. The most successful people choose not to give time to hate.

When we hate we are giving away something that is precious; our thoughts and our time. To whom are we giving this precious, personal gift? The very person we say we hate! It's like rewarding someone for having hurt us!
It is hard to let go of pain and it is only human to experience the strong emotion of hate. You feel that if you forgive someone, you are saying that what they did to hurt you is acceptable and of course, it isn't.

The only person you have to forgive is yourself for allowing hatred to take over your life. Put this strong, debilitating emotion away and treat yourself with kindness and respect. Understand that hate is ugly and ugliness has no place in your life.

Love yourself enough to get rid of hate. This life is yours; don't give it away to the emotion of hate one second longer.

Nourishing Thought:
~ Mitch Albom, author Tuesdays With Morrie When you hate, the object of your hatred has full control of your life. Do not allow anyone or anything to have that power. You deserve better.

8. Time Shouldn't Be Your Enemy, Make Friends with the Clock

This is the story of two men, equally successful in their field, but completely different in outlook and self-love. I worked with both of them and recently ran into them at a black-tie magazine awards dinner.

One man used to run his day by the clock. He had a schedule that he said allowed him to get everything done, thereby making sure he got nothing done that he wanted to do. He sacrificed all his time and energy to "tasks." Enjoyment for him would come, he said, "When I have time for me."
To this day, he still hasn't found the time for himself.

The other man worked hard but had one unbreakable rule during his workday. He was unavailable for anything during the hour he took for his lunch. He referred to it as "my moment." Those sixty minutes were his and his alone to do with as he pleased; they were reserved for his needs. He would go for walks in the park, look at nature, and listen to classical music. Whatever he did during that hour he did for himself and the time was all his. He once said that those moments were magical in helping him see the beauty that was all around him. It brought him a clarity of what was important to him, and he came back from that hour refreshed. He's still enjoying "his time" today.

We all have had periods in our lives when we rush through the day going from one thing to another, never stopping to take a breath before we move onto something else. Living like that is unavoidable at times, but to live that way every single day of our adult lives is life wasting and short-sighted.

In the vast scheme of things, we are given a short period to spend as we see fit. Even if we live to be one hundred, if we don't make time for small pleasures, we have wasted the years. Yes, work and life tasks take up a lot of our twenty-four hours but taking time for yourself to see the simplest beauty around you refreshes and renews your spirit.

Nourishing Thought:
"If I am not for myself; who will be? If not now; when?"
~ Talmud
Give yourself at least one "magical hour" a day to truly see the beauty
that can refresh your soul.

9. Forget the Number, Buy What Fits

"The best advice I ever received about clothes was from a designer. She told me to forget the size on the tag and buy what fits me. I am glad to say she's right!"

This advice applies to everything, not just clothes. Whatever makes you feel comfortable is what fits. Friends, spouses, jobs; choose what is the right fit for your life and good for you. Your life choices should reflect your desires. If you do something to please someone else, it will never be a perfect fit for you. Don't become a doctor because that is what you are told you should be if you want to be a teacher; don't live in Minneapolis if you love Florida heat. Whatever fits you makes your life happy.

The same goes for relationships. The man or woman you seek to spend your life with should be a "good fit." This isn't to say that you can't be individuals, but each person should complement the other. A healthy relationship should never become a second full-time job. A good fit for you is one where you're comfortable in all areas of your life.

Find what fits you best and make small changes if something doesn't. Clean out the closet of life and dispose of anything that makes you unhappy or no longer fits your idea of being happy. Forget the size and go for the fit.

Nourishing Thought:
"Alter the dress to fit madame, not madame to match the dress."

Balenciaga, haute couture designer to his fitting staff Life is too short to wear the wrong size. Make sure you're comfortable in your world. Be satisfied to satisfy yourself.

10. Use the Good Japanese

"The good Japanese and crystal should be reserved for company only."

A little quiz:
Do you have "good" things kept in a closet which you'll use "someday?" Are the good Japanese and crystal used only for the company? What does that tell you about how you see yourself?

By not using our very best items for ourselves, we're saying that we're not worthy of the best. In essence, we are diminishing our lives by not having the pleasure of the wonderful things we would not hesitate to offer to others. Why do we treat ourselves so shabbily?

My Aunt May had what she called a secret vice. She bought the softest, most beautiful French silk sheets she could find. She had a linen closet full of these leaves in a lovely variety of pastel colors, and she used every single one of them. Aunt May enjoyed sleeping on those beautiful sheets for years.
Her sister-in-law once accused her of being extravagant and asked her why May needed the silk sheets when cotton was what "other" people had.
My aunt replied that she didn't need them, she wanted them.
"If I don't indulge myself in this manner then I'm saying that my life isn't worth sleeping on silk sheets. The sheets are a metaphor for self-worth and a celebration of me. My life is deserving of silk sheets."

Nourishing Thought:
"What are you waiting for?! Open the bottle of expensive perfume and live!" Coco Chanel Don't treat your life as second best. Celebrate you! Sleep on silk sheets and use the good china.

11. Release Guilt and Embrace the Divine

"Unless it can change your life, guilt is the most useless emotion we have." ~ Cicero **We are amazing creatures, we humans.** We hold onto guilt and wear it like Hester Prynne wore the scarlet letter in Hawthorne's famous book. We wallow in it; we develop a relationship with it, keeping it with us night and day. Guilt becomes our constant companion stopping us from living the healthy and abundant life we need to live.

Some people think that by feeling guilty, they are showing an acceptance of their responsibility in a matter, but that is far from the truth. The only good that will come from guilt is if it can positively change your life. If you feel guilty that your behavior may have hurt someone, even inadvertently, resolve to stop the behavior. Apologize if necessary, then let go of the guilt. Holding on to it will only hold you back from living.

We have all done things in the life of which we are certainly not proud. We have unintentionally hurt others and ourselves. But unless we were deliberately cruel, the only thing we are guilty of is being human, and humans are not perfect.

Forgiveness of self is one of the most important things you can do for your life. Without that self-forgiveness, you cannot hope to live a full and happy life. The roadblocks to happiness were put up by you, and you are the only one who can remove them. Hating yourself is an emotional illness.

There is a spark of the Divine in all of us. A friend of mine from India once explained that the typical Hindu greeting of namaste, accompanied by hands joined together and a slight bow of the head, means,
"That which is of the God in me greets that which is of the God in you."
How beautiful a greeting!
That spark of the Divine is what we embrace when we learn to forgive ourselves. Forgiveness of self is a divine and compassionate act.

Nourishing Thought:
"Guilt is anger directed at ourselves. Stop being so damn angry." ~ F. Scott Fitzgerald See the Divine in you. Namaste!

12. Society and the Myth of Self-Sacrifice

Society is based on a system of beliefs, and most of those beliefs come from religions. One of the most disturbing of those beliefs has come down to us from the time of the Puritans. The belief is that suffering will buy us something. In the case of the Puritans, people were made to believe that unless they suffered, they could not gain entrance to heaven. Suffering supposedly bought them that admittance.

The vestige of self-sacrifice and suffering for others is still with us today. The person who sacrifices self is seen as a noble human being while anyone who puts self first is considered to be selfish. Even in the 21st century, this antiquated way of thinking influences us in our lives. The media, movies, literature; all celebrate the person who sacrifices their wants and postpones their dreams to put the needs of others first.

But that way of thinking is wrong. Suffering only buys one thing: more suffering. There's nothing noble or excellent in leading a life of misery. Despite numerous ideas to the contrary, you are not put on earth to lead a life of suffering. Your life should be a reflection of inner harmony that allows you, through your abundance and love of self, to give something back to the world without taking anything away from yourself.

Helping others is not enhanced by our suffering. You need a positive, compassionate nature to be of service to others. Who are you helping if you are suffering? Not yourself and certainly not anyone else. Every minute of your life is a precious gift. Self-imposed suffering and sacrifice dull and tarnishes the gift.

Nourishing Thought:
"Self-development is a higher duty than self-sacrifice."
~ Elizabeth Cady Stanton, social activist Do not sacrifice you; you are all you have.

13. Becoming You: Purpose of Vision

"I walked like Cary Grant, I talked like Cary Grant, and, eventually.....
I became Cary Grant!"

 On my desk, there is a framed saying that I cherish. It says,
"You are not what you were born, but what you have it in yourself to become."
That saying reflects the way I learned to live my life. If I had followed what some "well-meaning" people told me I should do with my life, I would have stayed in a working
environment, as well as a marriage, where I was miserable and the "real me" would have been
buried. I would not have done what I wanted and needed to do: Become me.
Who do you want to be? This isn't just a question that guidance counselors ask high school
Students in a senior year. This is a question you should ask yourself. In the case of a man named
Archibald Leach, born in abject poverty, the answer was that he wanted a much better life, a life
Of abundance and happiness. He found it when he became Cary Grant. He had a purpose of
vision.
Simply defined, the purpose of image is what you want and how you want to live. Doing something just because others have done so before you or because you have been told that that is what you should do is not in your best self-interest.
Decide exactly what you want to do with your life by asking yourself these questions. **Who** do I want to be?
How do I want to live?
What talents do I have that will help me achieve goals?
Even something as simple as insisting on being called by your name, instead of a nickname you always disliked, can help you become the person you want to be. Name changes are only part of the process of becoming you. A particular lifestyle, a different style of dress, a new career; all contribute to the "you" you want to be. The choices are yours.

Nourishing Thought:
"To successfully reinvent yourself, it is important to be flexible."
~ Vivian Diller, Ph.D., NYC
The creative work that goes into becoming 'you' is a gift to the world and to every being you meet.

14. Loving You, Loving Another

"The finest thing in the world is in knowing how to belong to oneself."
   Before we can actually love another person, we must love ourselves. This may seem a simple thing to do, but it isn't. The media is filled with images of romantic couples, and we are made to feel something is not right with us if we aren't part of a couple.

While loving and being loved is one of the most unusual experiences that can happen to us, we need to own our lives before we merge with another's. Know who you are, where you are, and what you want your life to be before committing to another. This isn't to say that you can't socialize or test the relationship waters; you don't have to be a hermit. But self-love gives you certain rights and one of these is the right to be with a person who respects and honors you as you deserve.

The best relationships are those which begin with liking each other, mutual respect, and honoring each person's dreams. Loving another entirely can only come from a love of self. Loving yourself teaches you how to love another.

Nourishing Thought:
"Love yourself first, and everything else falls into line. You have to love yourself to get anything done in this world." ~ Lucille Ball, comedian, actor, businesswoman
By loving yourself first, you learn to understand the concept of love fully.

15. Money and Happiness: the Real Connection

"The secret to using money to buy happiness is to spend money in ways that support your
happiness goals." ~ Gretchen Rubin, best-selling author

Nourishing yourself means that you have goals. A certain amount of money is necessary to have the lifestyle you choose for yourself.

This comment goes against just about every sentence ever written about happiness and money, but it true. If you spend your money in ways that help you reach a goal that adds to your happiness, then you have spent that money wisely and nourished yourself well.

It is a paradox that our society, on the one hand, shows lavish lifestyles of wealthy people in the media while on the other it is subtly hinted to the rest of us that having money equates to being a miserly, cruel Scrooge of a human being. This is so far from the truth. Money does not turn you into an evil person. A real man is enhanced by having money and gives back to society through philanthropy.

The real connection between money and happiness is what it can buy you to make your dreams come true or make your life better. If your dream is to write the next great novel or become an artist whose work appears in galleries, let the money from your current job make you a patron of the arts: your art. It takes money to pursue a goal. Support your dreams.

For practical purposes, money buys peace of mind such as a home security system or a safer car. It can help you stay healthy through proper nutrition and care. Using it well enhances your life. Going on a brief vacation to relax and revive your senses is good for you, body, mind, and soul. It is not money wasted.

Used in active ways, money buys what will support your happiness goals. It should be one active, healthy aspect of your life.

Nourishing Thought:
"Money isn't evil when you use it to make your life stable and
healthier."

~ Larry David, co-creator of Seinfeld Money spent on a goal or dream
is never wasted. Let money support your dreams and aspirations. Be
your patron of happiness.

CONCLUSION

Through this journey, I looked for any positive sayings that would strengthen me and help you find your way. I have compiled the sayings along with the wisdom I have learned on my journey, into a book to help others learn to live an active and fulfilling life. Thank you for purchasing this book I hope you will apply the acquired knowledge productively.